Accessing ... Citizenship: Crime and Justice

Bhavini Algarra

Acknowledgements

The photographs and artwork are reproduced by permission of the following (from top to bottom, left to right): p. 4 © Neil Reed, Allied Artists; © Rex Features; © Sipa Press/Rex Features; p. 5 © Action Press/Rex Features; © Rex Features; © Heathcliff O'Malley/Rex Features; © Sipa Press/Rex Features; pp. 6–7 all artwork © Mark Stacey; pp. 10–11 © Nicholas Bailey/Rex Features; © Alex Segre/Rex Features; artwork © Pete Roberts, Allied Artists; pp. 12–13 all photos © Greater Manchester Police, except woman police officer with two children © Alamy/Photofusion; p. 14 © Metropolitan Police; p. 15 © Greater Manchester Police; © Nigel R. Barklie/Rex Features; p. 16 graphics © Norwich Union and Crime Concern; pp. 17–18 © Gary Andrews, Allied Artists; p. 19 graphics © Norwich Union and Crime Concern ; pp. 22–23 all photos © HM Prison Service Museum, Newbold Revel, Rugby, UK; pp. 24–25 all photos © Ginny Lindenbaum; p. 27 © John Dillow, Beehive Illustration; pp. 28–31 © Gary Andrews, Allied Artists; p. 32 © The Howard League for Penal Reform; p. 33 © The Howard League for Penal Reform; youth looking out of window, modelled for The Children's Society; pregnant woman © Ginny Lindenbaum; prison population graph © The Howard League for Penal Reform; p. 34 © Crown Copyright. NMR; © Graham Kennedy, Allied Artists; © Neil Reed, Allied Artists; © Graham Kennedy, Allied Artists; p. 35 Grendon Prison artwork installation © Roger Perkins; p. 36 © Graham Kennedy, Allied Artists; p. 37 © MLA Press 2004; © Pete Roberts, Allied Artists; p. 38 © Gary Andrews, Allied Artists; p. 39 © Graham Kennedy, Allied Artists; p. 40 Neil Reed, Allied Artists; p. 41 Gary Andrews, Allied Artists, pp. 42–43 Pete Roberts, Allied Artists; p. 44 © Theresa Tibbets, Beehive Illustration; p. 45 © Crown Copyright. NMR; © Crown Copyright. NMR; pp. 46–47 CCTV © Greater Manchester Police; timer switch © Sue Sharp; marking property © Greater Manchester Police; all artwork © John Dillow, Beehive Illustration.

© 2004 Folens Limited, on behalf of the author.

United Kingdom: Folens Publishers, Apex Business Centre, Boscombe Road, Dunstable, LU5 4RL.
Email: folens@folens.com

Ireland: Folens Publishers, Greenhills Road, Tallaght, Dublin 24.
Email: info@folens.ie

Poland: JUKA, ul. Renesansowa 38, Warsaw 01-905.

Folens publications are protected by international copyright laws. All rights are reserved. The copyright of all materials in this publication, except where otherwise stated, remains the property of the publisher and authors. No part of this publication may be reproduced, stored in a retrieval system, or transmitted, in any form or by any means, for whatever purpose, without the written permission of Folens Limited.

Bhavini Algarra hereby asserts her moral right to be identified as the author of this work in accordance with the Copyright, Designs and Patents Act 1988.

Editor: Louise Titley
Layout artist: Kim Sillitoe
Cover design: 2i Design / Cover image: Corbis
Page design: Kim Sillitoe

First published 2004 by Folens Limited.

Every effort has been made to contact copyright holders of material used in this publication. If any copyright holder has been overlooked, we should be pleased to make any necessary arrangements.

British Library Cataloguing in Publication Data. A catalogue record for this publication is available from the British Library.

ISBN 1 84303 566 9

Contents

Law and Order

Why do we have laws?	4
Criminal acts... who's breaking the law?	6
Criminal and civil law... what's the difference?	8
'I'll see you in court!'... But which one?	10

Policing

Policing today	12
Reducing crime... focus on Stop and Search	14

Crime and Punishment?

Does crime pay?	16
What punishment?	22
Life behind bars	24
Anti-social behaviour orders... is this the way forward?	26
Is there justice?	28
The Howard League for Penal Reform	32
Is there an alternative?... Focus on Grendon Prison	34
The Youth Justice System	38
Why do young people break the law?	40
Caught committing a crime?... What happens next?	41
The youth court	42
Found guilty in court?... What can happen	44
Young offenders' insitutions	45

Preventing crime	46
Want to know more?	48

Law and Order

Why do we have laws?

BREAKING NEWS...

The anarchists believe in the power of the people to run their own lives without interference.

What happens next?

Law and Order

Criminal acts...

- Which of these people is breaking a law?
- Why do you think each law exists?
- Should there be some new laws introduced?
- Should some laws be scrapped?

Read on… and make your own mind up!

a Jim is 23 and has bought a bottle of whisky to drink at home tonight with his girlfriend.

e Amanda is 16 and has been helping her dad on the farm. He lets her drive the tractor home.

b Jim's younger brother, Alex, who is 13 years old, is at home too and Jim lets him have some of the whisky.

f When they get home Amanda realises she has left her bag in the barn. Her dad lets her drive the car back to get it.

c The following day, Alex, who has discovered a liking for drinking whisky, goes to the off-licence with his brother's ID to buy a bottle for himself. The shop owner believes the ID belongs to Alex and so serves him.

g Gary and Ben are gay and are having a sexual relationship. They are both 16 years old.

d The following week Alex goes to another off-licence. This time he doesn't have his brother's ID and he still has his school uniform on. It's obvious he's still at school but the shop owner sells him a bottle of whisky anyway.

h Gary's younger sister, Jane, is 15 and is having sex with her 17-year-old boyfriend, Rashid.

...who's breaking the law?

i Ben's twin brother, Mike, is secretly having a sexual relationship with a friend of his older sister. The woman, Mandy, is 47 years old.

n Lisa has no money, and is very hungry. She is in a sweetshop when she notices the cashier go out to the stockroom for a moment. Lisa sticks a bar of chocolate in her pocket.

j Narinder is 11 and she has just bought a pet rat from the local pet shop. She saved up her pocket money for a month.

k Narinder's mother, Jaspreet, has decided that a rat is an inappropriate pet for a little girl and so goes to the market and buys her a tortoise.

o Lisa's dad works for big bank. He is in charge of transferring billions of pounds a year all over the world. For the past five years he has been creaming a bit off each transaction and has now built up over a million pounds in a secret bank account.

l Marten is 22 years old and lives in Amsterdam. He has come to London to visit his friend Simon. While clubbing they buy some marijuana from someone who approaches them there.

p Lisa's uncle has no such luck; he has debts, no job and very few prospects. He agrees to join a gang who are going to break into a pub after a busy Saturday night and help themselves to the takings.

m The following month Simon goes to Amsterdam to visit Marten. They go out to a coffee bar where the owner offers to sell them a spliff. They choose some good quality marijuana to smoke before they go out to a club.

Law and Order

Criminal and civil law…

Which is which… a criminal or civil case?

'Sexist' Schroder pays out £1.4m in compensation

A City analyst who claimed she was forced to quit her job as a result of sex discrimination is to receive £1.4m in compensation after Schroder Securities dropped an appeal against the record payout.

Julie Bower, a £120,000 a year former drinks sector analyst, told an employment tribunal last year that she was paid an 'insultingly low' £25,000 bonus while two male colleagues received £650,000 and £440,000.

© *Guardian*, Julia Finch, 20 June 2002

Copycat singer loses fight over song

Robbie Williams' latest album may be called *Sing When You're Winning*, but there was little evidence of either yesterday when the former Take That star lost an expensive copyright battle.

© *Guardian*, Keith Perry, 3 October 2000

WORLD'S WORST INTERNET PERVERT
and he gets just **FIVE** years

© *Daily Mirror*, 10 October 2003

DOG KILLS BABY BOY
Pet attacks as 'drunk' childminder sleeps

© *Daily Mirror*, 21 May 2003

JAIL FOR TRUANT'S MOTHER

© *Daily Mirror*

Civil law

Civil law deals with disputes between individuals and groups. The person who has been injured or has suffered loss as the result of a wrong that only directly affected them, generally brings a civil action. Civil law cases are often about one's rights being abused. Usually the claim will be for compensation.

Areas covered by civil law are:

- copyright or intellectual property disputes: for example, music sampling, or plagiarism (copying someone else's material and passing it off as your own)
- property: boundary disputes, trespass
- work-related disputes: unfair dismissal, personal injury
- defamation of character: saying false things about someone
- consumer disputes: faulty goods, 'trades description' offences

...what's the difference?

Criminal law

Criminal law deals with disputes between an individual and the general public. A criminal offence generally refers to behaviour that breaks the rule governing society. Criminal cases such as murder are brought by the Crown Prosecution Service, which represents all citizens, against the offender. The principal function of criminal proceedings is to punish the offender.

CAPTURED
Bin Bag suspect held at Great Ormond Street last night ... hours after CCTV caught him trying to get drugs at another hospital

© *Daily Mirror*

I'LL PROTECT THEM
Becks ups security after kidnap shock

© *Daily Mirror*

CRACKDOWN
EXCLUSIVE: WE JOIN BRITAIN'S TOUGHEST DRUGS SQUAD ... BUSTING THE CRACK HOUSES

© *Daily Mirror*

Neighbours' £150,000 fight over six-inch strip of land

© *Daily Mail*, 11 November 2003

OUT OF CONTROL
This 11-year-old girl has been arrested 30 times ... another day in lawless Britain

© *The Mirror*

I AM WIRED
Brit shoe bomber's chilling threat as he tried to blow up jet

© *The Mirror*

Law and Order

'I'll see you in court!'...

Both civil and criminal cases are heard within their own court system. Each court has its own procedure and practice.

Inside a magistrates' court

...But which one?

Inside a crown court

Policing

Policing today

The police do not make laws; they enforce them. The laws are there to protect the public.

A position of responsibility

The police play a vital part in:

1. supporting victims and witnesses,
2. providing reassurance and confidence to individuals subjected to crime,
3. protecting the public from incivility and anti-social behaviour.

Policing

Reducing crime…

Does Stop and Search work?

> **"Being stopped by the police can be a hassle…**
> …but I understand what they're trying to do, to cut down on street robberies and people carrying weapons."

To make the streets safer, the police sometimes have to stop people and ask them to account for their actions or presence in an area.

As the police want to be open, honest and accountable, they will now provide a record explaining why a stop or a search was carried out.

For more information about Recommendation 61 go to:

www.met.police.uk/stopandsearch

METROPOLITAN POLICE — Working for a safer London

...focus on Stop and Search

Crime and punishment?

Does crime pay?

Crime Concern, an independent organisation working to reduce crime, and Norwich Union, an insurance company, carried out some research about crime and young people. In July 2003, 510 young people throughout the UK aged 13 to 19 were interviewed. A further 138 interviews were conducted with young people living in socially deprived areas in Chester, Hackney and Birmingham during August 2003.

What did they discover?

In socially deprived areas, crime is part of the fabric of many young people's lives: 94 per cent of teens have experienced crime.

Over 80 per cent of those interviewed knew someone who had been involved in crime.

In the London Borough of Hackney, one in three teens revealed they had experience of gun crime.

Young people would like to see the police doing more to reduce crime.

Crime and punishment?

Does crime pay?

On a national level over 40 per cent of young people feel that crime does pay and within socially deprived areas this figure rises to almost 60 per cent.

For many teenagers the material benefits of crime outweigh the risks of punishment or even the punishment itself.

When asked who they most respected, the majority of young people, 64 per cent, named their parents. In socially deprived areas, 49 per cent of teens named their mother as the person they most respect.

The government and its views are too far removed from young people's day-to-day lives according to
• 84 per cent of young people.

Fear of crime

- Not worried by crime 12%
- Accept crime is part of society 33%
- Concerned I or friends and family may be victims of crime 55%

Young people's role models

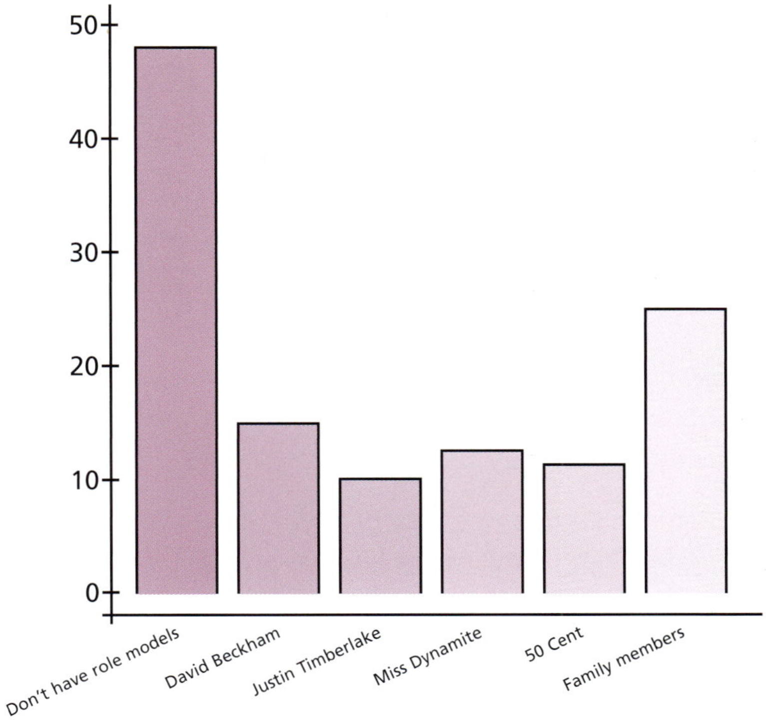

Category	Value
Don't have role models	48
David Beckham	15
Justin Timberlake	10
Miss Dynamite	12.5
50 Cent	11
Family members	25

Most effective deterrents to crime

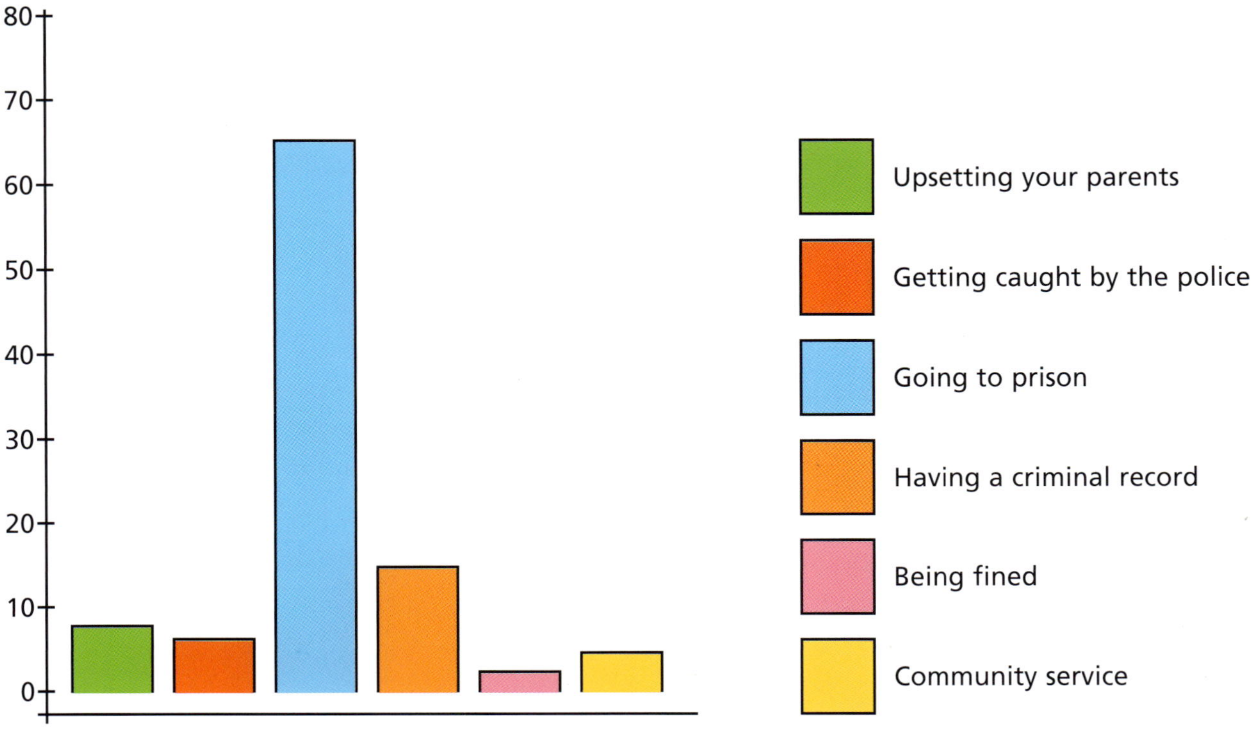

- Upsetting your parents — ~8
- Getting caught by the police — ~6
- Going to prison — ~65
- Having a criminal record — ~15
- Being fined — ~2
- Community service — ~5

Crime and punishment?

Does crime pay?

What do all the headlines have in common?

Crime does pay, say teenagers

About half of youngsters believe that crime does pay, according to a new report.

Four in 10 teenagers believe the material benefits of crime outweigh the possible consequences, even a jail sentence – and in socially deprived areas such as Hackney the figure increases to 60 per cent. More than 80 per cent of children interviewed said they knew someone who had been involved in crime. In Hackney, one in three had experience of gun crime.

© *London Evening Standard*, by Rebecca Mowling, 15 September 2003

Youngsters believe crime does pay

More than half the young people in Birmingham believe crime does pay and prison does not deter them from breaking the law, according to a survey published yesterday.

New research into young people's experiences of crime in the city revealed 58 per cent thought the material benefits of crime outweighed the consequences.

© *Birmingham Evening Post*, 17 September 2003

CRIME PAYS SAY TEENS

Teenagers believe that crime does pay, it was revealed yesterday. Norwich Union are working with the national crime reduction organisation Crime Concern on an anti-crime apprenticeship scheme where youngsters help to set up crime reduction schemes in their own communities.

© *Daily Mirror*, 16 September 2003

DEPRIVED TEENAGERS BELIEVE CRIME PAYS

The findings are part of a report; Youth Insight, from insurance company Norwich Union and Crime Concern which runs a scheme that has seen three apprentices work with Crime Concern managers to implement crime reduction schemes.

© *Young People Now*, 17 September 2003
http://www.ypnmagazine.co.uk

Crime and punishment?

What punishment?

If you commit a criminal offence you should be punished. But how?

Criminals were put in the **stocks** as a form of public shame. While in the stocks, members of the public could throw rotten vegetables and stones at them.

The **scaffold** at Gloucester Prison. The scaffold was used to hang prisoners who were sentenced to death.

A jailer supervising prisoners on a **treadmill** at Gloucester Prison, c. 1900. Prisoners were expected to do 50 steps a minute, that meant climbing up to around 6 km a day uphill.

Jailers used **shackles** and **manacles** on prisoners from the 1200s. The jailers would charge the prisoners to remove the shackles and manacles.

The body of a hanged criminal would be displayed in a public place in **gibbet irons**. This was done to deter other budding criminals.

Crime and punishment?

Life behind bars

Today the majority of convicted criminals are sent to prison. Over 63,000 people live behind bars in Britain. Are we too hard on our criminals or, as the tabloid headlines frequently suggest, too soft? And more importantly: does prison ever work?

Crime and punishment?

Anti-social behaviour orders…

The ASBO (Anti-social behaviour order) was introduced in 1999 in what was hailed as a Government 'zero-tolerance' policy.

Dob on a yob!

The *Daily News* invites you to name and shame anyone from your neighbourhood who is making your life hell with their anti-social behaviour.

Rat on a rat

Your local police force invites you to 'shop' anyone you know who is involved in joyriding, theft or other anti-social behaviour in your area.

...is this the way forward?

Gang named and shamed

In a rundown area of Brackton, the streets have suddenly become peaceful and happy places once more. Senior citizens and mothers with young children are now happy and confident to walk to their local shops again.

This is a dramatic change, from just a few weeks ago, when residents of the area lived in fear of the local 'Preston Street Gang' who terrorised the neighbourhood with their abusive, violent and anti-social behaviour. In an unusual step, the local police force named and shamed the members of the gang – and they are now subject to a mass anti-social behaviour order, which bans them from local streets.

Crime and punishment?

Is there justice?

The robbery victim

28

Disrupting criminals

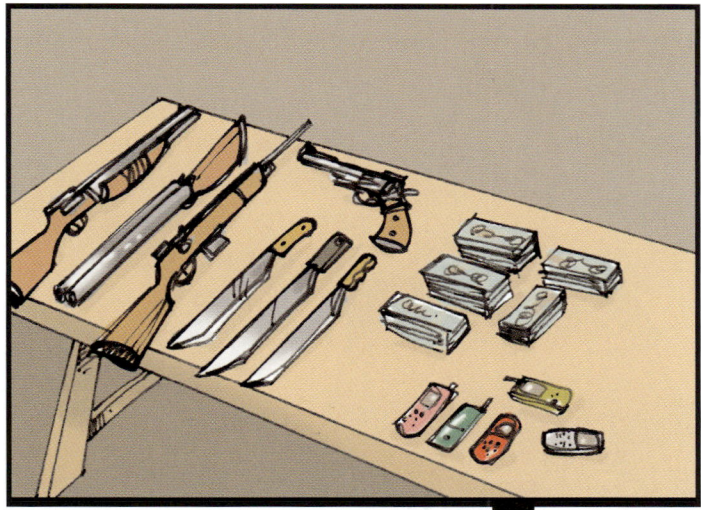

Crime and punishment?

Is there justice?

Tackling domestic violence

The elderly victim

Crime and punishment?

The Howard League for Penal Reform

the **Howard League** for **Penal Reform**

About the Howard League for Penal Reform

- The Howard League for Penal Reform is the oldest penal reform charity in the UK.
- It was established in 1866 and is named after John Howard.
- The Howard League for Penal Reform is entirely independent of government and is wholly funded by voluntary donations.

John Howard was vitally important in the development of the international penal reform movement, and the importance of his life and work is reflected in this inscription on his statue in St Paul's Cathedral.

'This extraordinary man had the fortune to be honoured whilst living, in the manner which his virtues deserved: he received the thanks of both houses of the British and Irish Parliaments, for his eminent services rendered to his country and to mankind.'

Howard League for Penal Reform Campaigns

The Howard League for Penal Reform believes that prison should be reserved for serious and violent offenders, and that there are more effective ways of responding to anti-social behaviour through restoring the damage done by crime.

Community service, probation, fines and the new sentences for young people involving their families and victims offer cheap and effective solutions.

Current campaigns

Graph showing prison population

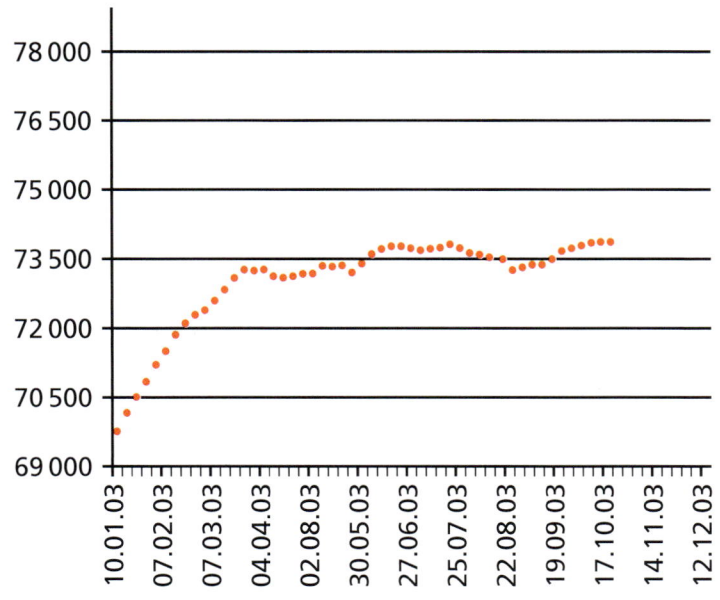

Children's rights

Prisoners with special needs

Girls in prison

Prison overcrowding

Suicide and self-injury prevention

Crime and punishment?

Is there an alternative?...

Grendon doesn't look any different from any other prison: it's faceless with loops of razor wire along its outer fences that keep the community inside apart from us outside. However, inside it *is* different…

You could find this type of message inside the Christmas cards in the Governor's office:

'Thank you for giving me this chance to change.'
'I don't have long to go now until I'm released. I am very confident about me and my future.'

Grendon is unique. It is a 'therapeutic' prison. This means that the inmates are not only confronted with their crimes but, more importantly, are encouraged to seek other, more positive, ways to deal with their behavioural problems. The inmates are all serving long-term sentences for serious crimes.

...Focus on Grendon Prison

Grendon Prison – ongoing artwork installation

◀ **Each box contains a personal possession of an inmate.**

Grendon inmates were asked to choose an object or possession of theirs that they felt connected them to their idea of 'home'. This could be a past home, a future one, or their present one in prison. They were also asked to provide a short statement explaining why they had chosen the object they had donated.

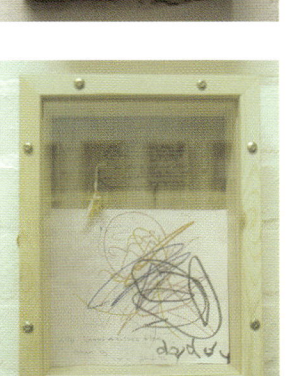
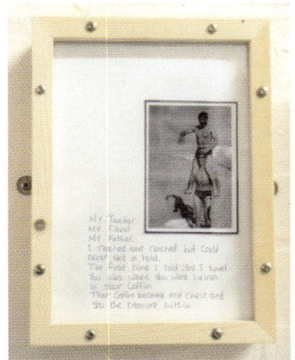
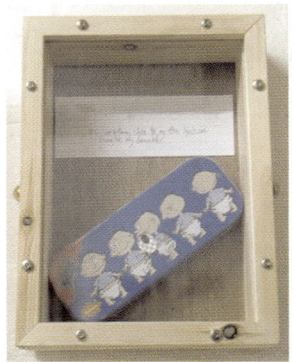

Crime and punishment?

Is there an alternative?...

Who's inside Grendon Prison?

All of Grendon's inmates had to personally volunteer to be sent there.

95% have committed violent offences

27% have committed sex offences

94 of the men are serving life sentences

...Focus on Grendon Prison

Real stories

Not everyone will leave Grendon a changed person, but many inmates do undergo a radical change. It is hoped that they will be less aggressive, less hostile, less dangerous and less likely to reoffend.

Mark Leech said, 'It certainly worked for me. Once you get locked into being a criminal, you just accept it. Grendon made me realise there were other options I could choose.'

Mark Leech spent 20 years in 62 different prisons. But since Grendon he has become an award-winning writer and leading campaigner for penal reform.

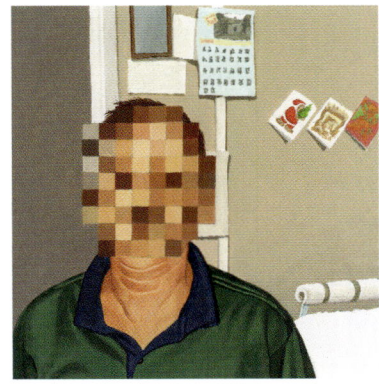

'My name is Sean. I'm 37 and am serving a life sentence for rape. I've spent time in many prisons around the country. I want to turn my back on crime. I committed the rape. That was the point in my life when I thought I had to do something. I couldn't go on like that. Grendon has taught me how to deal with people, how to communicate. Before, I could not see the victims. Now I can. In other prisons it was me against the system. Here I feel I'm part of a team who are working towards my progress.'

'My name is Daryl. I'm 35 and am serving 10 years for conspiracy to commit an armed robbery. I'd been a thief all my life. When I got nicked for this I thought to myself, I've got to try and sort my life out. I was sick of my own behaviour, but I didn't know how to break away from it. Grendon has given me another chance. You have to do things you never thought you would do here. I believe in myself this time. I want it. That's the most important thing. You've got to want it.'

From: Prison – the Therapeutic Way, © *Guardian*, Sally Weale, 2 February, 2001.

Crime and punishment?

The Youth Justice System

The Youth Justice System is based on the idea of restorative justice.

Three main objectives are:

1 Responsibility

2 Restoration

3 Reintegration

The present system was set up by the Crime and Disorder Act 1998 and the Criminal Evidence Act 1999.

Two new bodies were created:

1 The Youth Justice Board

2 The Youth Offending Teams (YOTs)

Crime and punishment?

Why do young people break the law?

Not getting on well at school or being bullied

Drugs or alcohol

Harsh discipline at home

Trying to show off

Boredom

Caught committing a crime?... What happens next?

If it's a first or minor offence...

You plead guilty...

Warnings have no effect... the Youth Offending Team is called upon...

The YOT will continue to work together until a programme of rehabilitation has been decided upon.

If it's a serious offence, or the youth keeps re-offending, it is time to go to court.

Crime and punishment?

The youth court

Witness: a police officer or another person might give an account of the incident. Witnesses only attend if the young person charged pleads not guilty.

Magistrates: two or three magistrates sit behind a bench. They are women and men from the community, not lawyers. It is up to them to decide whether the young person is guilty or not and how they are going to be dealt with. Most magistrates are not paid.

The **young person**, their parents and solicitor: the young person charged sits in the middle of the court in front of the bench.

The **usher**: the usher calls in the witnesses and keeps out members of the public who are not allowed in.

Youth Offending Team: some of the team may come. They sit at the back of the court.

Crime and punishment?

Found guilty in court?...

Three options can then follow...

A *reparation order* can be made, instructing the offender to apologise to the victim, or make reparation for the crime they have committed.

An *action plan order* can be made, in which the Youth Offending Team draws up a three-month community work plan with offender.

A *custodial detention and training order* can be made. Under 15s are taken to a local authority secure unit. Over 15s are taken to a young offenders' institution.

...What can happen?

Young offenders' institutions

Outside Lancaster Farms Young Offenders' Institution.

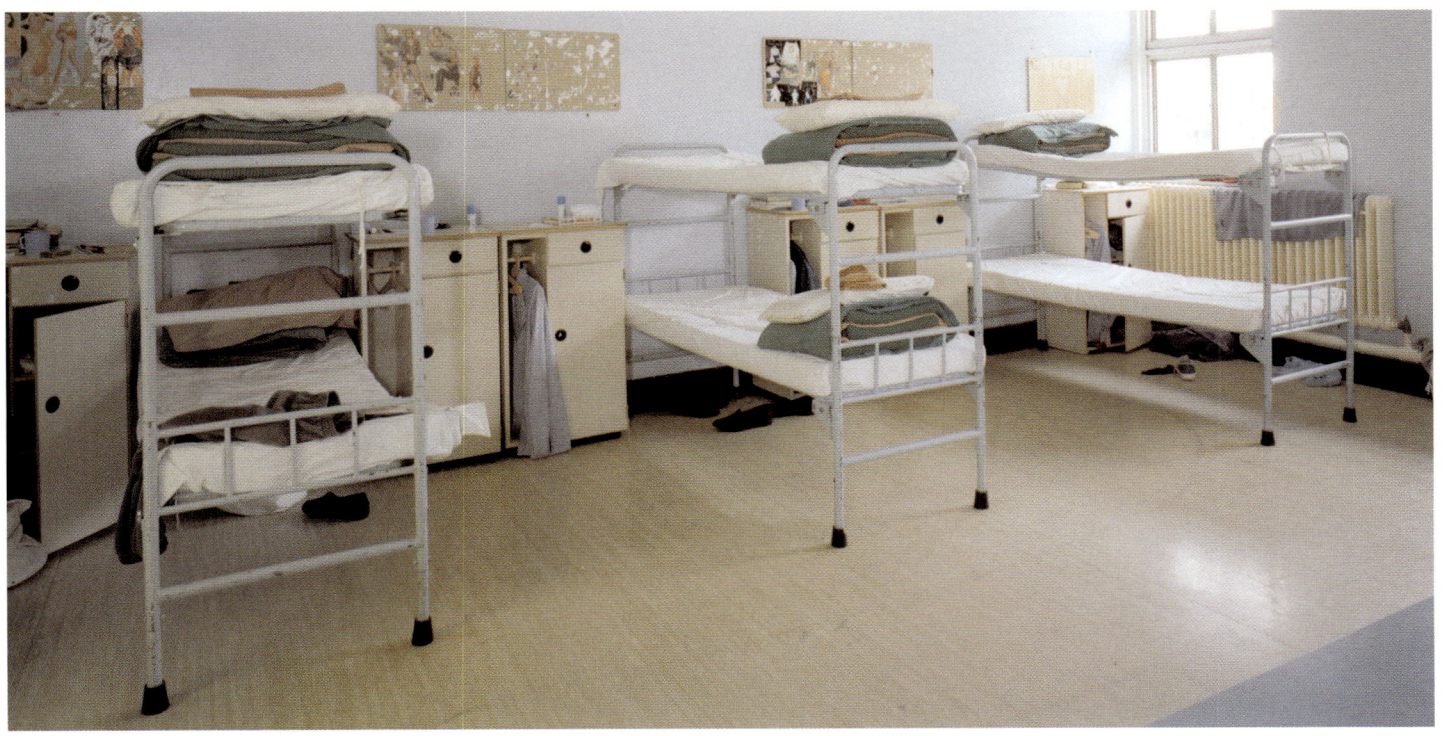

Inside a dormitory at Dover Young Offenders' Institution.

Preventing crime

Want to know more?

Her Majesty's Prison Service: www.hmprisonservice.gov.uk

Crime Concern: www.crimeconcern.org.uk

Children's Society: www.childrenssociety.org.uk

Inside Out Trust: www.inside-out.org.uk

Justice: www.justice.org.uk

Nacro: www.nacro.org.uk

Prisoners' Education Trust: www.prisonerseducation.org

Victim Support: www.victimsupport.org.uk

Inquest: www.inquest.org.uk

Criminal Justice System: www.cjsonline.org

Women in Prison: www.womeninprison.org.uk

crimeinfo: www.crimeinfo.org.uk

Action for Prisoners' Families: www.prisonersfamilieshelpline.org.uk